Mastodons

poems by

Daphne Rose Ewing

Edited by Deborah L. Fruchey
Afterword by Karen Ewing

Last Laugh Productions
Walnut Creek, CA

ISBN: 979-8-9899369-5-3
Library of Congress Control Number: 2025902560

Book Design: Deborah L. Fruchey

Cover Art:
Bing Image Creator, with the prompt,
"Mastodon as seen in a dream."
Back cover:
Unknown photographer, Daphne and David at Daphne's birthday
lunch 4-25-22; digitized by Josh Love; with permission

www.lastlaughproductions.org
logo by Bradley Stockwell

Dedication:

To Daphne Rose, with love:
in memory of a crucial day in 1979,
when you talked me out of taking my own life.
Gratitude forever, and may God bless you
in the hereafter

And to Karen Ewing,
who worked so hard to locate
more recent poems,
and gave me much comfort

TABLE OF CONTENTS

Early Poems

Sometimes in the Night.. 1
Price Tags.. 2
36 Cups of Coffee... 3
What Was... 4
Paradoxically Yours... 5
The Tie that Binds... 6
Murder in Iambic Pentameter... 7
Pretending... 8
Ode to Bodies of Visible Vapor... 9
Of Steel & Velvet...10
Vicious Cycles...11
Chance Meeting...12
Relative to the Observer...13
Smokey..14
Come Again?...15
Dreampeople...16
For the Vampire...17
Epistle Concerning Whatever it Was I Said to You........18
Rainmaking...19
Killing Ourselves...20
Morbid Curiosity..21
On Maintaining Images and Taking Oneself
     too Seriously...22
Sonnet for the Songwriter 1971...23
Last Will and Testament...24
Retraction..25
Mastodons..26
A Realization Made too Late...27
Father of the Bride...28
You Can't Win...29
A Commoner's Observation...30
Paper Dolls...31
Psychokinesis as a Manual Means of Motivation..........32
Mobius Clockwork in ¾ Time..33
The Mathematics of Abnormal Psychology...................34

To Arms!..35
A Toast to the Cardboard Man.....................................36
Newsbreak..37
The Madwoman's Anthem..38
A Matter of Relocation.......................................39
The Cardboard Man (reprise)......................................40
Untitled Lie..41
Designated in the Absence of Light............................42
To Daddy...43
The Art of the Plainsong..44
Circa 1968...45
Compass Points..46
The Neurotic's Approach to Haute Couture.................47
No Time Like the Present..48
Laundry as it Relates to the Socio-Economic
    Climate..49
To No One..50

In Memorium...51
Poetry from Last Laugh Productions............................53

Sometimes in the Night

Sometimes in the night
When the stars show their faces
And the moon puts in an appearance,
I recall
Good times,
Better days, finer hours when life
                              Was life
              Not merely time intersecting with
                  Space in
                              The aether.

I recall
Your eyes,
Innocent but learning, accumulating voluminous quantities
Of knowledge;
Wise but understanding, knowing my weaknesses
And being kind enough to accept me for myself.
There were times
        When there were no hours
        Only the meeting of two minds
        Interlaced in meditation.
        There was hope,
        There was love (friendship might be more
Commonly understood, but it was love also).
And all these things
Come to mind
When I'm alone,
When the stars show their faces
When the moon puts in an appearance,
Sometimes in the night.

Price Tags

I said a phrase one day, it seems,
And since that time it haunts my dreams.
And even though I pray and cry
I'll pay for words until I die.
For words will fall (like night or rain),
But though time passes, words remain...

36 Cups of Coffee
(The speed of thought)

the loneliness in crowds
the night —
light —
     hopes —
         dreams —
the starvation in spirit —
the end of beginnings —
hunger
for freedom —
     the pain —
         enduring —
the inventions of madness —
     within walls —
         without plans —

     question

What Was
(for KC)

We lived in a world we built ourselves
Because this one didn't fit;
It was old
And broken, in a state of disrepair.
Ours was new and unexplored and wild;
And in all the mad countryside
There were only we two.
And we were happy;
Oh, we did make occasional voyages back to the
Old world for the benefit of
                    Others,
Outsiders who didn't know and wouldn't have cared
If they did.
Then we would return —
It was forever different and eternally changing,
Making metamorphosis into —
              Into what?
We never had the chance to know.
We never had the chance to be.
It's only me, now,
And although I'm not by myself,

I am.

Paradoxically Yours

Too close — so far from me;
Too loud — I cannot hear you;
Too dim — light blinds me;
Too dear — yet strangers;
There must be solution — there is none.
There must be discussion — there is none.
There must be decision — there is none.
      I'm no good at salvaging decaying
Relationships;
      I don't know how to repair the damage,
How to make the pieces fit,
      And so

It goes,
      Distances too vast to trek in a lifetime
Face me, light years of disappointment to
Cross
      Before
  I will know...
Too strong — so frail;
Too young — a thousand years of dues paid;
Too scared — drawn to you;
Too settled —
      And yet
            So lost
                  In space
              And
           Time

The Tie that Binds

Would that I could
      Unremember you;
If I could unsee you, would I? I search for
Ways in which to
            Unlove,
But memory clings tightly.
Endeavoring to unthink,
Struggling to unneed;
            I feel close to crying.
            I live in fear that I will,
            And you will see. Once
            A tear falls,
            It cannot be
            Unwept...
My life cannot be unlived,
Nor can I go back and uncreate the twisted
Dream,
            Unwish the absurd hope.
Would that I could
      Unwant,
That I could unfeel the sorrow,
      Undo the shackles that bind me to you
(Keeping me away at the same time)
Would that I could
      Unshare common bonds,
      Unsay certain truths,
            Unpromise

Yet if I could,
I would be so much poorer
For unknowing
You.

Murder in Iambic Pentameter

Your image fades — you start to walk away:
I have no right to try and make you stay;
I know I have no claim upon your heart,
But, even so, inside I'm torn apart.
You turn to leave — I'm forced to stay behind.
I'm glad you don't know half what's on my mind,
For if you did, I know you'd be distressed
To see the tortured love that I've suppressed.
I'm sorry: there's so much I'd like to do,
But I've no right in reaching out to you;
And I've no right in hoping you will see
What really constitutes the inner me.
You move from me — I want to touch your hand,
But truly fear that you'd misunderstand.
I want to love you, want that love returned,
But there's no love as far as you're concerned.
I dream of future times, what could have been,
But love was killed before it could begin
To take hold; now there's no chance it will grow:
If you must leave, then kill me as you go.

Pretending

The woman of no man's dreams
Stares out open windows
Measuring the night
By her own darkness

Ode to Bodies of Visible Vapor

I like the rain and I'll tell you why:
    When the sun is covered by some variety of
Cloud, it calls to me of the past when
    The entire world was that way.
It hearkens of
The dim time
When there was warmth indoors, security
Against the continual storm.
Now when I see the dark riders approach
Across the horizon, I remember
And I let the sky
Do my crying for me.

Of Steel and Velvet

So thoroughly mellow: a tower of power:
Can solve any problem if given an hour;
She knows what she's after, she takes what she wants
With what-the-hell devil-may-care nonchalance.

So calm and collected: if she's forced to duel
She'll cut you to ribbons without being cruel;
You can't get her ruffled, but you make demands
And you will have taken your life in your hands.

Decidedly level: accustomed to winning,
She's been in control from the very beginning
She's cool and she's lethal — she knows her own mind
And does what she wants when she feels so inclined.

The rock of Gibraltar: she's got it together;
There isn't a hurricane she couldn't weather,
A woman of action: not easy to take —
It's really too bad her whole life is a fake.

Vicious Circles

I build you up,
You slap my face;
When you're accused
I plead your case.
When I'm on trial
You're never there
And you've the gall
To say you care.
You laugh at me
Behind my back
And tell my friends
The things I lack.
As time goes by
I clearly see
How you have lost
Your need for me.
But on we go
In tortured rhyme:
Less help than hurt
Most of the time.
I hold your hand,
You bruise my arm:
There's little hope
And so much harm.
I need to breathe,
You need to grow,
We need to live:
Please let me go.

The Chance Meeting

You must think I followed you here;
Let me dismiss that idea right now.
It's merely coincidental that we had to be
At exactly the same place
At exactly the same time
And the fact that
You mean the world to me is irrelevant.
So if you'll excuse me
Now that I've seen (fortuitously, albeit)
The face I love so much
I'll be on my way.

Relative to the Observer

Two women passed each other by
And each, pretending not to see,
Surveying with a narrow eye,
Was caught up in her vanity.
Each smiled a smile that was subdued
Because she thought herself more fair;
Assured, again, of pulchritude,
Each passed the other unaware.
And so it seems to be the rule;
That man condemns and man exalts;
At best, he's cold — at worst, he's cruel
In dealing with another's faults.

Smokey

I have seen the silver tiger
Creeping soft through carpet jungles
Waiting for the proper moment
When the victim will be sighted
Silver claws and golden lanterns
Will soon flash in lamp-lit forests
And the battle will be ended
While the tiger purrs, victorious.

Come Again?

Did I hear you correctly?
I must be in error
Because
I thought you said you cared
  And I know beyond
  A shadow of a doubt
No sane, rational human being involves
Him or herself
In others' lives nowadays.
Affection is in poor taste,
Love is abhorrent and
Compassion is out of the question
To the educated mind.
So I'll allow you to repeat
   Yourself
For the benefit
Of my
  Faulty hearing.

Dreampeople

Dreampeopleliveinsmoglesssuburbansplitlevel
homesgoingouttoexpensiverestaurantssocializing
constantlymakingenviablefriendshipsandfalling
inpermanentlovewithperfectloversjettingto
Majorcawhenthespiritmovesthemneverowing
moneytoanyonelivingdeadorotherwiseengaged
dreampeopleneverdietorshavetheirlegsandmake
mejealousbecausetheyneverhavetotakeoutthe
trash

For the Vampire

There's a full moon out tonight
And those who fear the werewolf will be cowering
    In their beds behind bolted doors.
But there are no werewolves.
There *are* vampires.
I am reminded of this as I see you smile.

Epistle concerning whatever it was I said to you in my dreams last night and did not mean despite the way I behaved

Words lost
In morning
Cut so deeply
By starlight.
I saw and did not see you cry.

Rainmaking

Evening falls softly,
   Starless windows,
   We make moonlight.
Endeavoring to be tender,
I whisper and you hear me.

Sunlight comes creeping,
   Golden silence
   We make morning.
I wonder as you turn your head in that
Certain way which signifies impending
Alienation

Afternoon bright vanished,
   Swathed in dimness,
   We make rain.
Forgo the conventional folderol —
Tell me truthfully,
Was it ever real?

     I thought not.

Killing Ourselves

Here we sit in an almost-lighted living room
Pretending we have things to say
And remember how to laugh.
But I'm no fool
And I'm more than well aware of
How dead we are.

Morbid Curiosity
(there are two sides to every nightmare)

Goodnight, Rose.
Today they laid you lowly, clad in black,
Where you will sleep in the deepness.
I wish that I had known you
But you never truly
Existed.
Goodnight, Rose.
I wish we could have been together
But I was not myself from the start
And now you've gone
Before you've arrived.
We shall not meet
And from the dark you will cry out to me in
Silence
And no one will fill your absent space.
You died before you were ever born
And it will eternally haunt me:
I wonder who we would have been.
Goodnight, Rose.

On Maintaining Images and Taking Oneself Too Seriously to the Point of Self-Deification

Today he questioned my divinity
So I sent a lightning bolt
      Which promptly struck him dead
      Where he stood.
Good riddance.
We of obvious perfection
Can do without the peons of this world
(With the exception of their worship...occasionally).
But, somehow,
I miss him
      Which is irrespective of the fact
That he was only mortal
And I dwell upon Mount Olympus
(Having seen to it that the former tenants
Were evicted after the proper thirty-day
Notice).
You see, he questioned my divinity
      And I did away with him.

So much
      For my
Devoted
      Congregation.

A Sonnet for the Songwriter 1971

Your gaze cannot be met for there's one thing
I have not said despite the fact you cared;
The lacerations tell me when they sting
That I'd have done more for you had I dared.

A lidded eye, a clenched fist — that is me
Or, rather, what I deem a proper face;
I can't allow myself to truly see
For feelings lead to downfall and disgrace.

I said you'd changed; I made you take the blame
For all the wrongs of which I was the cause.
You put up no resistance, bearing shame
As if you loved me more for all my flaws.

I pushed you back (a deed which I denied);
I said I never loved you... and I lied.

Last Will and Testament
(for whoever it may happen to apply to)

I have a last request or two
To state here before leaving;
You see, I plan to move along.
I'm tired of deceiving
Myself and friends and foes alike:
It's only me I'm killing
And now that I have reached this point
The panic is distilling.
I want to leave with you a thought,
That being I adored you
Despite the fact I often cried
And many times I bored you.
But as it is, I'm on my way
And bid you only kindness
For there were times when only you
Could touch and cure my blindness.
Some years from now I'll cross your mind
When once you stop to ponder;
I hope by then when I appear
The greeting will be fonder.
But memories will crumble in
The way which time disposes;
When I have gone please bury me
With daphne and with roses.

Retraction

You used to write love letters on notebook paper;
I used to believe them
Until the day I saw
The ink slowly
Vanish

Mastodons

No, I don't hallucinate
Although occasionally I do see
                    Mastodons.
Is that so bad?
They're not pink; they're average over-the-counter
Bargain-basement garden-variety
            Primitive pachyderms
            That could use Dial.
But really, I have no delusions;
Can I help it if the behemoths surface only for me?
It's rather hard to ignore
A living thing two stories high which
Smells like a beached whale and is
Peeking over your shoulder.
Imagine being stepped on by this nonentity —
Imagine never imagining again!

So I maintain I don't hallucinate — I only
See mastodons

        Which makes a great deal more sense
        Than seeing some of the people
        I am told I see
                Every day.

A Realization Made Too Late

While no one knew the meaning of life,
I did.
No one could support their beliefs,
& they stood helpless.
I did not.
But I have no goals.
They do.
I want nothing.
They do not.
>So here I stand with my answers
>And ethics which only proves that
>I shall experience
>More intelligent
>Insanity.

Father of the Bride

When I look back
How clearly I remember
Wearing white
And wishing
Lightning would strike the far end of the
      Front pew
And then strike
      Me.

You Can't Win

O the judgement day's nearing
As the downtown smog's clearing
And the cities of earth will be leveled;
The designers conspired to see we're "well-attired"
(Even fools can see we look disheveled).
The fat cats in high places with the memorable faces
Wouldn't last on a boulevard urban;
It does my poor heart wonders when I think that oil blunders
Are the fault of some punk in a turban.
So in my indecision I seek television
To be told half the world's busy dying
While the other half's looting and destroying and shooting
Can you figure? I've given up trying.
There's congressional smearings culminating in hearings
In the name of an item called justice;
Guilty pleas and repentance equal suspended sentence
(We don't trust them and they hardly trust us).
I don't know how you see this but if you're asking me this
I would say that these wrongs won't be righted;
We can hardly erase it and we might as well face it
That the turds of the world have united.

A Commoner's Observation

She's a Paris original:
Fashion with footprints,
Aplomb with artistry:
I watch
From secure distances
As she floats
Above the pawns of everyday life.
She doesn't *have* style — she *is* class;
Those of us written
In lower case letters
Can only observe
And wish.

Paper Dolls

We stand in measured rows
Chorusing platitudes
We have learned
And have come to believe.
No need to wonder;
We grin foolishly
Because we are to be happy
Subsisting on the drivel of life.
Seek unification no longer —
It's here, brethren,
As we hold hands
And blow away
In the breeze...

Psychokinesis as a Manual Means of Motivation

You move without moving,
Without being near you are present
And it's all because
I wished so hard
That I see you floating
Out the window
     And it's a long, long way
     To the ground

Mobius Clockwork in ¾ Time

Vision: there is only the omnipresent, devouring
NOW,
And we walk the treadmill suspended above the
Void of all our cotton-candy dreams and wishes.
So airy —
They are wisps left to us, a legacy of the temporal.
We wad Time up, tear it down and recreate
Pretended moments
        To simulate self-fulfillment,
        To pacify the anger,
        To quell the shame of misfortune.
Divide, mark and catalog your ill-gotten gains as
It pleases you;
As for me, I am tired
And there are so many yesterdays
In my future.

The Mathematics of Abnormal Psychology

One plus one equals stupidity.
One plus one equals endless compromising
To the point of lost identity.

One plus one equals three which equals
 One divided by one which equals

            Nothing

To Arms!

Why don't we fight about it?
I'll tell you what:
You organize your aerial reconnaissance
And I'll activate my nuclear warheads
And we'll end this Mexican standoff
Like the four-star
Dyed-in-the-wool idiots
We really are.

A Toast to the Cardboard Man

So here's to you, my pretty one,
And here's to all the lies
And here's to the hypocrisies
Describing you defies;
And here's to all the special times
You left when things got rough
And here's to what you weren't to me
When you weren't there enough.
A wish for you, my pretty one;
A girl description fails,
A lovely thing to teach to you
Those things heart break entails.
She'll never leave you, pretty one,
Her worth you'll not contest;
So here's to what the future brings.
You — you deserve the best.

Newsbreak

You see what happened was it just got to
be too much for her you see but I don't
know all the details but they say she
just cracked up and did the most shameful
things but like I said I only heard this
from my friend Sally who knows a cousin
of her next-door-neighbor and she said it
was all true and she should know you
see she was a funny sort to begin with
and they say

The Madwoman's Anthem

I keep thinking there must be a why
But how would I know?
Someone somewhere froths wisdom at the mouth
Rescuing the reprobates of society with a magic word —
I think —
But how would I know?
There is a rumor that contract negotiations
        Between Man & Woman
Have reached a satisfactory conclusion.
I don't think it's true.
But how would I know?
          I believe it's time
          To flip a coin.

A Matter of Relocation

Now we live in Relative Obscurity
You know
In a split-level daydream
As a result of schizophrenic land-use-planning.
You must come visit sometime
And let us show you the town.
It takes awhile to find it
But once you get there
You're gone.

The Cardboard Man
(reprise)

I looked in your eyes
   And
There was nobody home.

Untitled Lie

I dream of years:
The godless days when,
                Wandering,
        I led myself astray.
No matter,
The beginning is at hand,
And the end
As we come full circle...
A choir of one,
I serenade the seasons.
I dream of years:
I sing the song again.

Designated in the Absence of Light

O, clever liar, how you haunt me still
In dreams by dark, in murderous thoughts by day:
You may have changed your shape to suit your will
But it's exceeding clear you've come to stay.
There is no reason given for this plan
Which, based on sheer emotion and not fact,
Contends that you are but a different man —
Still, pain remains the price you would exact.
If there were words to write what went before,
If there were time to tell you what could be,
If there were patience left to love you more
You would not understand if you could see.

I seek your gaze and, as if by design,
The empty eyes which meet my own are mine.

To Daddy

The reason I miss you
Is simple:
You were
Never
Here.

The Art of the Plainsong

O, God our Father,
Forgive our foolish trespasses
And be Thou ever near to bring much needed
Punishment and Chastening to
Errant members of the Flock.
Thy rod and Thy staff, they comfort us,
When administered unto our deserving fellows.
O, God our Father,
Second verse,
Same as the first.

Circa 1968

This is the song that no one will hear:
I will keep it within me for always.
When I wander at night through the hallways,
I'll sing it to me.

This is the song that no one will sing:
When I look in the night through my window,
I can see all my thoughts in the wind blow —
And hold back the tears.

Do you know what it's like to be locked
Up inside?
And do you know that some things
Can't be denied?

This is the song that no one need know:
When I look late tonight in my mirror,
I will see all the emptiness clearer;
I'll lie down and die.
Goodbye

Compass Points

See the seagulls on my roof;
I am nowhere near the ocean.
You say you think they must be misguided.
Consider, if you will, the proximity
Of the heart to the mind
And perhaps such distances will seem
Insignificant.
See it rain on the poor, stupid birds;
Perhaps it is so evenly grey in their world
That they have lost all sense of direction.
It happens sometimes as I, for one,
Can attest.
Fly in circles and you will become dizzy
And be no nearer your destination
Than your point of departure.
See the cat on the doorstep,
Waiting.

The Neurotic's Approach to Haute Couture

Get this:
I've almost become used to wearing self-pity
As a regular part of my attire.
It's rather like having shit on the bottom of your shoe
As you stand packed too tightly to move on the bus
Behind a stalled tractor-trailer
Halfway across Ross Island during the commuter rush.
There's simply no graceful way to be rid of it.
So I scuffle along
And everyone is well aware of the problem.
Some laugh, some pretend not to notice,
Some have had it happen to them before,
Yet no one moves.
So I scuffle along,
Sticking to the pavement and
Cursing this jumping-off point
Between the realities.

No Time Like the Present

I hate you because I love you and
You don't know it,
And if I tell you, you will reject me
And if you reject me
Then I will hate you,
So I think I'd better start hating you now
And avoid the rush later.

Laundry as it Relates to the Socio-Economic Climate of Modern America

Socks are destined
For bachelorhood,
But sheets mate for life.

To No One

Sometimes I sit and think of death.
I contemplate its meaning
On moonlit nights such as this one
When winds are loudly keening.

I analyze the aftermath,
Survived by those about me.
What will they say?
Will they mourn long
Or get along without me?

I trace my fingers on the glass
And try to come to reason
With too-short days, the passing weeks,
Each brief and fleeting season,

And feel the fire that is my life
Fade to its final ember.
What's left of me when I have gone
Will be what you remember.

In Memorium
April 24, 1955 — December 18, 2024

It is with great sorrow that I report the passing of Daphne Rose Ewing. While there is a medical cause for her death, I believe she died of a broken heart after losing the love of her life, David Ewing, the one she waited 45 years for — after meeting him in college. After the zigs and zags of their respective lives, they reconnected and didn't waste any time being together for what they both said were the best eight years of their lives. She adored David, as he did her.

Life can be both beautiful and brutal. This year it was both. After losing David in July, we walked through his passing and the weeks and months following his death alongside Daphne, who quickly became family — my sister.

Daphne was a beautiful soul. She chose joy and life even amid the disappointments of an imperfect fate. She was interesting to talk to and interested in those she was talking with. In my experience her focus was outward, more than inward. These traits allowed her to have and maintain deep friendships. I am grateful to those with whom I have connected.

Daphne had a successful career as a technical and proposal writer. She was intelligent and a good communicator.

While her final months (only five) without David were grief filled, she wasn't in despair. She was beginning to make plans, and updated her resumé. But it wasn't to be...

Rest in peace, Daphne.

Karen Ewing
January 2025
Excerpted from the Facebook post

Editor's Note:

The poems left to us were composed before 1986; they are reproduced here in a font that reminds me of her rounded, exceptionally clear handwriting. Tragically, it appears that her mature work has been lost...the foregoing was mostly written before she had her son, Christopher. Daphne had agreed to publish in 2023, but was not well enough to follow up, as she suffered from Long COVID.

Other Poetry from Last Laugh Productions

The Nearest Place Distant, by Stephen Francis Cosgrove

Hint, by Deborah L. Fruchey

What Still Matters, by Johanna Ely

We'll Always Have Stockton, by Steve Arntson

For Whoever Thinks a Piano is Furniture, by Rudy Jon Tanner

The Hall of Painted Sonnets, Sonnets by Steve Arnston, Art by Diane Lee Moomey

Embodied, by Jan Dederick

Armageddon Bootcamp, by Maria Rosales

Bat Flower: poems, plays, and other perversions, by Vampyre Mike Kassel

Three Kinds of Dark, by Deborah L. Fruchey